# The Happiness Connection
## The Bible & The Brain

CHRISTINE SCHADER

ISBN: 0692927115
ISBN 13: 9780692927113
Library of Congress Control Number: 2017910619
CreateSpace Independent Publishing Platform
North Charleston, South Carolina

Cover Design Inspiration:


~ SOME SEE A WEED, SOME SEE A *WISH* ~


Scatter *HAPPINESS...*

To My Amazing Friend,

Always remember you are worthy, deserving and YOU
ARE ENOUGH!

~ Written with much Love and Appreciation ~

Shine On!

Hugs and Happiness,
Christine

# ACKNOWLEDGMENTS

This book is the result of many, many astonishing individuals. I've been so blessed to have incredibly inspiring teachers, mentors, coaches, experts, friends, and family in my life who have taught me the power and possibilities of expanding love and happiness. Because of you, this book became a reality. Please accept this manuscript as my thank-you!

I want to further acknowledge the following:

Of course—though He probably goes without mentioning—I want to acknowledge, first and foremost, God. Through God's Grace and vast love, all things are possible. Through my love for and from God and the great teachings of the Bible, I was spiritually inspired to write this book. I felt it was an actual calling, what I call a *God whisper.*

I also want to acknowledge my hubby, truly the wind beneath my wings. Throughout our thirty-four plus years of marriage, my husband has been my biggest cheerleader. He has believed in me even when I didn't believe in myself. He has loved me even when I didn't feel lovable. He has encouraged me, built me up, and reminded me that anything is possible. Because of his commitment to our relationship, we have withstood many ebbs and flows, which has taught me the value of persistence. He continually demonstrates what love is on a daily basis, and I am so blessed. I appreciate you so!

I am grateful for my kiddos—they are amazing, brilliant, talented, and beautiful; they really are, I'm not just saying that because I'm their mom. My greatest lesson in love has come from these beautiful souls. Unconditional love for these beings has taught me more about the pure strength and power of love than anything else. It has helped me realize, as best I can, the limitlessness of God's love.

I recently had the opportunity to take two powerful courses that helped in the development of this book. Both instructors said it was their deepest desire that this information be shared as much as possible so they could see the ripple effects in the world. I believe God placed them in just the right spot at just the right time.

Over the years, I've had the incredible opportunity of working together with various wellness programs with-in several organizations. These companies have incredible foresight and such appreciation for their employee's well-being, that they offer workshops on health, wealth and happiness, as well as, one-on-one coaching at little or no cost for their employees. It was during a wellness program planning sessions that I had the pleasure of being introduced to Dr. Daniel Hayes, PhD. "Dr. D" (as I like to call him) also provides workshops through the wellness department. Consequently, I had the opportunity to take his nearly yearlong program on stress management; as a result he brought a calm to my world when it was much needed. He has been a confidant, sounding board, and inspiration. Thank you Daniel—I'm not sure you realize the value you brought into my life. I'm forever thankful!

I also recently had the absolute delight of taking a Happy on Purpose (HOP) course and having Leslie Villelli, a happiness co-creator and life coach, as my personal happiness coach for over a year. The year was transformative, to say the least. As a coach myself, I'm a firm believer in the empowerment of coaching and continually strive to gain inspiration, gentle prodding, and accountability from others on a regular basis. Leslie's love, dedication, and direction helped shape many of the teachings in this book. Thank you!

This book would not have materialized if not for the encouragement of professional writer Karen Hayes. Karen gave me the belief that I could do it. Through her reassurance that I was on the right track, that I could indeed finish this book, and that my "genuine heartfelt message" was worth being heard, this book came about. Karen did all of that from her generous, gracious, and kind heart. I'm so grateful!

Acknowledgments                               vii

1   My Journey                                  1
2   In the Beginning                            6
3   Happiness is…Our "Soul" Purpose            12
4   How to Be Happier                          18
5   Intentional Happiness                      23
6   WTF? Growing Happiness                     37
7   Clearly Happy                              47
8   The Magic of Happiness                     65
9   Shopping for Happiness                     77
10  Designed for Happiness                     81
11  Happily Mindful                            85
12  The Happiness Connection                   89
13  Peacefully Happy                           97
14  The Biology of Happiness                  103
15  Happily Grateful                          115
16  Holding Happiness                         120
17  Ultimate Happiness                        123

In Conclusion                                129
Author Biography                             131

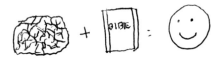

# 1

# MY JOURNEY

I'm not an expert on either the Bible or the brain. I'm simply a girl who found her way back to God through love and in the process discovered her happiness again.

My heartfelt desire as you read these pages is that you will discover expanding love, peace, hope and happiness through the lessons shared throughout this book. These principles are a compilation of my thirty years of extensive studies in both the mind and spirit and working with thousands of clients.

I've designed this book to be a used as a workbook. A book for you to use for added insight to what brings you happiness and joy. Please write in the book, highlight, earmark pages, put notes in the margins, doodle, draw, star, and use the notes sections to write anything you want to remember, anything that resonates with you, anything you'd like to learn more about and anything you want to apply to your life. The more you mark up, write and apply, the more meaningful the teachings will be. There is magic when you put pen to paper, so scribble away.

Let the journey begin...

I grew up going to various churches, mainly Baptist (as that was the Sunday school bus that picked me up). But when my family went to church, we hopped around and went to various houses of worship. We attended our local Jewish synagogue, the Church of Jesus Christ of Latter-day Saints, Seventh-day Adventist, Unity, Catholic, and Methodist churches, and a variety of other churches. I loved church, summer Bible camp, and Bible school.

I treasured the community and the sense of belonging. I cherished being loved by God and I *love* **Loving** God. So, I embarked on my own study of theology to learn even more.

Searching for absolute understanding and answers in the Bible was frustrating. I wanted to separate politics and God. I wanted to separate the hierarchy. I wanted to believe in an all-loving God, not the judgmental and vengeful one I was often taught to be fearful of in church. I wanted to adore and love God and not doubt or be afraid. I desired verifiable evidence that the Bible was historically and scientifically accurate.

As a result of my studies, instead of feeling closer to God and church, I found myself beginning to doubt a lot of what I had originally been taught. I began wanting more and more proof. I questioned everything, and I had trouble finding answers. When I did come upon answers, they were often beyond my comprehension. It was so much easier just to have faith.

This journey left me with even more doubt and confusion and a conundrum as to what to believe. I found myself pulling away, and as a result I began to miss the comfort that faith and community bring.

I still believed in God. My spirituality never wavered. I still prayed and marveled at the miracles and blessings in my life, yet I felt somewhat disconnected and lost.

In my bewildered state, I noticed I wasn't as happy as I had been before my search for knowledge. I've since learned that many folks go through this struggle once they move past faith to wanting more evidence and verification.

So, in my attempt to add more happiness to my life and to fill some of the void I was feeling from lack of connection, I started studying positive psychology. That led me to study the brain, which led me to study neuroscience, particularly, neuroplasticity and epigenetics. Only then did I discover answers to many of my questions and realize that _it's science that has actually caught up to the teachings of the Bible_.

You see, as a life, happiness, and money coach with decades of experience helping clients achieve their goals, dreams, and desires, I already knew that most of how my clients handled money, relationships, and their lives had to do with psychology and how their brains were wired. I realized that if I developed their action plans around what brought them happiness and joy, they were much more likely to achieve their goals and add wealth to their portfolios. I started applying what I had learned from my studies of the brain and adding it to my coaching practice so I could teach others how to change their brains to change their lives.

In the process, I had an epiphany: What if the Bible was actually the first book on positive psychology, neuroscience, and the law of attraction?

People are hungry for more...more peace, more love, and more happiness. What if God gave us the Word as an actual instruction manual to help guide us toward realizing great happiness and love? What if it tutors us on the fundamentals of neuroscience, positive psychology, happiness, and well-being? What if it actually teaches us how we are biologically designed for happiness and many other great scientific truths?

I hope that by reading this book you will discover some of the answers to these questions. If this book can help just one person find a way back to God/Love and create more happiness and well-being in life, then it has served its purpose.

Chapter Notes ~ Highlights:

- Action plans should be based around happiness and joy
- The Bible is a book on positive psychology
- God can lead us to happiness

# 2

## IN THE BEGINNING

It all starts with the Word and Love!

In the beginning was the Word.

### John 1:1 (King James Bible)

*In the beginning was the Word, and the Word was
with God, and the Word was God.*

The Word was God!

### 1 John 4:8 (KJV)

*God is love; and he that dwelleth in love dwelleth in
God, and God in him.*

And God is Love!

If in the beginning was the Word, and God is Love,
then we should be able to substitute the word "Love" for

"God" (or "the Lord," "the Holy Spirit," and "Jesus," all of which are truly synonyms for "Love") at any time throughout the Bible (and life in general). If we do that, then even the most challenging scriptures become not about a vengeful God but about His love. They're not about threats and punishment but about care and guidance on how to enjoy life to the fullest.

Let me give an example. One of the most trying scriptures for me has always been Exodus 34:6–7 (GOD's WORD Translation):

> *Then he passed in front of Moses, calling out, "The LORD, the LORD, a compassionate and merciful God, patient, always faithful and ready to forgive. He continues to show his love to thousands of generations, forgiving wrongdoing, disobedience, and sin. He never lets the guilty go unpunished, punishing children and grandchildren for their parents' sins to the third and fourth generation."* (Emphasis mine)

Well, that certainly sounds like a punishing and threatening God. He is going to punish not only those who sin but also their children and their children's children as well! How is that fair? How is that just? How is that Love?

However, when I viewed this scripture through the lens of the latest scientific research, I realized it was actually a clue and warning, if you will, to guard us from going against Love by engaging in sin.

Sin is generally defined as any action or thought that goes against an ideal relationship with God/Love.

This is where the latest scientific research fits in. If you look at this scripture with a basic understanding of the most recent discoveries about our cellular structure and DNA in the field of epigenetics, then this scripture becomes all about guidance and love.

Epigenetics is a relatively new field of study that has shown just how adaptable our genes are to outside forces. That's right—the study of epigenetics has shown that external or environmental factors can basically switch your genes on and off and affect how your cells read genes instead of being caused solely by our DNA sequence.

Whoa! This is huge! We can change our actual cellular structure, for better or worse. We are not slaves to our DNA sequence.

Back to Exodus 34:7. Looking at it through the lens of epigenetics suggests that if you sin or go against Love, then you will potentially change gene activity and expression, which will have an effect on your children, your grandchildren, and so on. In the June 3, 2005 issue of *Science*, one of the more astonishing published reports suggested that epigenetic changes, which were once thought to last only throughout a single lifespan, may endure in at least four subsequent generations of organisms (remember in Exodus... *for their parents' sins to the third and fourth generation*). This is not about God being vengeful but rather about God guiding us in Love.

God's love for us is clear. It's not that He is demanding or punishing. He is actually trying to guide and lovingly teach us how our bodies and minds are already (scientifically) designed to work.

The Bible is full of scriptures about love, joy, and happiness. I believe the Bible is the Word to help us stay in love—with ourselves and others—and live purposefully happy lives. It helps to guide us toward manifesting our goals, dreams, and desires, and to live healthy, wealthy, and happy lives.

Likewise, the Bible is a manuscript to help us understand that should we move away from God/Love, then we move away from all that brings happiness, health, and wealth. God is Love!

### 1 John 4:7 (New International Version)

*Dear friends, let us love one another, for love comes from God. Everyone who loves has been born of God and knows God.*

### 1 John 4:8 (NIV)

*Whoever does not love does not know God, because God is love.*

### 1 John 4:16 (NIV)

*God is love. Whoever lives in love lives in God, and God in him.*

### John 13:34 (New Living Translation)

*So now I am giving you a new commandment: Love each other. Just as I have loved you, you should love each other.*

### 1 Corinthians 16:14 (New American Standard Bible)

*Let all that you do be done in love.*

Chapter Notes ~ Highlights:

_____

_____

_____

_____

_____

_____

_____

_____

_____

_____

_____

_____

_____

_____

_____

_____

_____

_____

_____

_____

_____

_____

_____

_____

_____

# 3

## HAPPINESS IS...OUR "SOUL" PURPOSE

I personally believe that our "soul" purpose in this world is to be happy. And I'm in good company...

The Dalai Lama agrees: "The purpose of our lives is to be happy."

Aristotle said, "Happiness is the meaning and purpose of life, the whole aim and end of human existence."

Our forefathers even wrote that our inalienable rights include "life, liberty, and the pursuit of happiness."

Happiness is also a gift from God.

### Ecclesiastes 3:12 (NIV)
*I know that there is nothing better for people than to be happy and to do good while they live.*

> *That each of them may eat and drink, and find*
> *satisfaction in all their toil—this is the gift of God.*

You are a child of God, and God wants you to be happy. He wants you to seize life and live to the fullest!

### *Ecclesiastes 9:7–9 (The Message)*
*Seize life! Eat bread with gusto,*
*Drink wine with a robust heart.*
*Oh yes—God takes pleasure in your pleasure!*
*Dress festively every morning.*
*Don't skimp on colors and scarves.*
*Relish life with the spouse you love*
*Each and every day of your precarious life.*
*Each day is God's gift. It's all you get in exchange*
*For the hard work of staying alive.*
*Make the most of each one!*

Happiness is not only good for you, it's good for the world as a whole. When you are happy, you help others around you feel happy. In other words, happiness is contagious. Happier people often make positive contributions to the world. Your happiness matters both for you and the world!

> *When I was 5 years old, my mother always told*
> *me that happiness was the key to life. When I went*
> *to school, they asked me what I wanted to be when*
> *I grew up. I wrote down 'happy'. They told me I*

*didn't understand the assignment, and I told them they didn't understand life.*

— *John Lennon*

Happiness is…

*Happiness is health and a short memory.*

—Attributed to Audrey Hepburn

*My happiness grows in direct proportion to my acceptance, and inverse proportion to my expectations.*

—Michael J. Fox

If your purpose in life is to be happy, then what exactly is happiness? How do you define happiness?

_____

_____

_____

_____

_____

As the quotes above indicate, and as you have surely discovered in your own pursuit of the meaning of happiness, happiness is different for everyone.

To illustrate, I often open a seminar by asking the audience, what their individual definition of happiness is. I skip around the room and ask folks if they'd like to share. I hear so many wonderful and different things – from my grandkids to my pup, from rain to sunshine, from the beach to the mountains, from peaceful retreats to rock concerts, from family and friends, to food, and so on.

People have told me cultivating happiness for others, while being of service often brings them happiness. That giving, feeling useful and making a difference creates happiness. That becoming our greatest version of self generates joy. That Love is what brings bliss. It is exquisite to watch each individual express what happiness means to them. Their faces brighten, their bodies soften, and joy exudes as they express what happiness is. The energy in the room expands, and you can actually feel the happiness radiating.

From this simple exercise you begin to see that ultimately, what brings happiness is absolutely individualized.

However, for the sake of this book, I am going to use the psychological definition of happiness:

> *In psychology, happiness is a mental or emotional state of well-being defined by positive or pleasant emotions ranging from contentment to intense joy.*

> -Wikipedia

How do you create a mental state of well-being, or any mental state for that matter? As you will discover in future chapters, it all starts with your thoughts!

*Happiness is not determined by what is happening around you but rather what's happening inside your mind.*

—Unknown

*Most folks are just about as happy as they make up their minds to be.*

—Abraham Lincoln

### *Psalms* 144:15 (KJV)
*Happy are the people whose God is the Lord.*

Remember, *God* is a synonym for *Love*. Therefore, happy are the people who Love!

God's desire is for you to live with great joy and love. As you will see in the following chapters, the Bible is full of guidance on how to do just that.

Chapter Notes ~ Highlights:

# 4

# HOW TO BE HAPPIER

Happiness is a skill. It's a practice. You actually have to train your brain for happiness by strengthening the neuropathways to fire for happiness.

The scientific community provides supporting evidence that it is primarily our thoughts that determine how happy we are. Science is finally catching up to the teachings in the Bible.

### Proverbs 23:7 (KJV)
*For as he thinketh in his heart, so is he.*

What you think you become. The foundation of our lives is built entirely on the thoughts we think.

## The Happiness Equation

Prominent positive-psychology researchers Sonja Lyubomirsky, Ken Sheldon, David Schkade, and Martin Seligman recently developed a scientific happiness formula:

$$H = S + C + V$$

Where H is happiness, S is a set point (i.e., genetic disposition), C is circumstances, and V is voluntary actions.

What percentage of your happiness do you think is derived from your conditions or circumstances...meaning your job, your bank account, your house, etc.? Seriously, what percentage do you think that is? Please write it down: _____%

Most people are under the misconception that their circumstances determine their happiness level, but actually, that is not correct. Believe it or not, your conditions only account for about 10 percent of your happiness. Once your basic needs are met, your money, home, job, and other circumstances do not contribute anymore to your overall happiness.

Many believe, "I'll be happy when (fill in the blank) happens." Get a job, lose ten pounds, find perfect mate. I call it the "I'll be happy when" syndrome. But just the opposite is true. Only when you're truly happy will all those things start to happen!

*Happiness isn't a crop that you harvest and your dreams come true. It's more like a fertilizer that makes them come true faster.*

—Unknown

The full happiness formula goes something like this:

Happiness = approximately 10% circumstances + approximately 50% set point + approximately 40% voluntary actions.

And remember, through epigenetics, it has now been proven that we can change our cellular expression (with the thoughts that we think and things that we do), so that means we can effectively change the 50% point as well.

I cannot emphasize how exciting this is! Imagine: up to 90 percent of your happiness is UP TO YOU!

*Very little is needed to make a happy life; it is all within yourself, in your way of thinking.*

—Marcus Aurelius

It all begins with your thoughts, and God has given you plenty of direction through biblical scriptures suggesting what you can focus on:

### Philippians 4:8 (NIV)

*Finally, brothers and sisters, whatever is true, whatever is noble, whatever is right, whatever is pure, whatever is lovely, whatever is admirable— if anything is excellent or praiseworthy—think about such things.*

Chapter Notes ~ Highlights:

# 5

## INTENTIONAL HAPPINESS

Scientific research has given even more clarity about how we can rewire the brain for happiness. With a basic understanding of neuroplasticity, we learn how our thoughts and words literally become reality.

Neuroplasticity shows that many aspects of the brain can be altered throughout life. Our brains are not just pre-programmed. They are not rigid and set but rather malleable like plastic. Scientific research teaches us that this neuroplastic change can happen when we change our behavior, environmental stimuli, thoughts, and emotions.

Simply stated this means that new situations, fresh thoughts, and a change in our environment can cause the brain to form new neural connections—they physically change and rewire the brain.

In other words, you can actually physically change and rewire your own brain simply by changing your thoughts.

Let's synthesize these scientific findings on neuroplasticity with what I shared earlier about epigenetics and our ability to change our gene expression through many of the same external factors. It becomes clear that, by choosing our thoughts and words *intentionally,* we can influence and ultimately actually determine our own interaction with the world; we can change our own reality.

You may wonder how this works. What you think becomes what you say, which becomes what you believe, which becomes how you act, which results in your life as a whole.

When I teach workshops on "The Happiness Connection", I start by sharing this research, because when I can scientifically show you that most of your happiness is up to you, that you are the author, star, and director of your story, that you are the architect of how your life turns out, then you begin to realize that you have control over creating intentional happiness for yourself. To a great extent you have the ability to write the ending of your story any way you like.

YOU can design and create the life you long for. For goodness' sake—not only that, but you have God and the entire universe on your side! The Bible tells us repeatedly that whatever we ask for and believe, we shall receive it.

### Mark 11:24 (NIV)
*Therefore I tell you, whatever you ask for in prayer, believe that you have received it, and it will be yours.*

Can God be any clearer? Ask, believe, and you shall receive.

Ask

### John 16:24 (NIV)
*Ask and you will receive, and your joy will be complete.*

### John 14:14 (ESV)
*If you ask me anything in my name, I will do it.*

It all begins with asking, using your own words. The Bible tells us how extraordinary and powerful words are:

### John 1:1 (KJV)
*In the beginning was the Word.*

In Genesis 1:3, God says, "Let there be light." God created all things with his Word. He literally spoke the world into being with the power of his words. And since we are created in God's image, we also speak life out of every thought we think and word we say.

### Ephesians 4:29 (ESV)

*Let no corrupting talk come out of your mouths, but only such as is good for building up, as fits the occasion, that it may give grace to those who hear.*

### Matthew 15:11 (NIV)

*What goes into someone's mouth does not defile them, but what comes out of their mouth that is what defiles them.*

### James 3:8–10 (ESV)

*But no human being can tame the tongue. It is a restless evil, full of deadly poison. With it we bless our Lord and Father, and with it we curse people who are made in the likeness of God. From the same mouth come blessing and cursing. My brothers, these things ought not to be so.*

Furthermore, scientists have discovered that our subconscious interprets what we say and think literally.

**So what does all this mean for YOU?**

You may want to consider carefully before speaking. **Ask yourself, is what you *say* what you want your life to *be*?**

Choose your words with care. Remind yourself that what you are about to say literally creates your life. This goes for self talk (the thoughts you tell yourself) as well. When you realize the absolute power that your words hold, you become more purposeful with what you say. Proverbs tells us that the tongue has the power of life and death, and I suggest that you start paying attention to what you are saying not only to others but to yourself as well.

You may want to consider changing how you use your words. Make positive and subtle changes in your vocabulary.

For an easy way to start, consider using a word like "fascinated" instead of "frustrated." Instead of "I have to," choose to say "I believe," "I choose," or "I get to." Change "I'm sorry" to "Thank you," as in "Thank you for allowing me time to arrive safely," instead of "I'm sorry I'm late." Consider changing "scared" to "excited". Did you know that fear and excitement produce nearly identical biological expressions in your body and often feel the same. How you choose to view it, is usually the deciding factor of whether you'll be anxious or in a state of anticipation.

Even these very small changes in how you speak and think will absolutely change your life.

Being deliberate with your thoughts and what you say, **creates a life by design instead of by default**. It's important to remember that **every thought you think and word you say is literally a direct prayer request to God**, therefore you'll want to be sure you align those thoughts and words with what you want in this world <u>not</u> on what you don't want. Your words are the beginning of the creation of your reality, the creative force in your life. For better or worse, what you say and the thoughts you think make an impact in your life. Hence, it is very important to be intentionally purposeful as we consciously choose our words and thoughts.

### Proverbs 16:24 (ESV)
*Gracious words are like a honeycomb, sweetness to the soul and health to the body.*

### Colossians 4:6 (ESV)
*Let your speech always be gracious, seasoned with salt, so that you may know how you ought to answer each person.*

Believe

### Matthew 21:22 (NIV)
*If you believe, you will receive whatever you ask for in prayer.*

The power of belief is what allows miracles to transpire. Ask, *believe*, and receive. The determining factor of whether something will be received is your belief that it will. In your beliefs lie the potential and magic.

Let me give an example of the power of believing. Before 1954, it was thought to be humanly impossible to run a mile in less than four minutes. Some medical experts even suggested that a person's lungs might explode in the attempt. On May 6, 1954, Rodger Bannister ran the miracle mile in 3:59:4. That set a world record. Which opened a new mindset and allowed other athletes to *believe* it was now possible for them to also break the record. As a result, today what was once thought impossible is continually achieved by many athletes.

### Mark 9:23 (KJV)
*If thou canst believe, all things are possible to him that believeth.*

### Matthew 9:29 (GWT)
*What you have believed will be done for you!*

A belief is something we accept as true. Beliefs are the thoughts that we tell ourselves over and over. Our beliefs will greatly influence whether something can *become* or not. For example, if you believe you cannot do something, you've already closed the door and you likely won't be able to do it. In some areas of our lives, it's time to challenge our beliefs. Are we thinking what we want to be thinking? Is what we are thinking creating happiness?

Your beliefs are both conscious and unconscious. Psychologist say that about 90% of our beliefs are actually subconscious. Therefore, it is extremely powerful to identify any subconscious limited beliefs that are getting in our way. One of the biggest limiting beliefs I found working with clients is that they have forgotten how big God is. They have placed limitations on God. They have put God in a "box". In my workshops I often show some of the latest photos from the Hubble satellite showing the astonishing size of the universe. From these photos, scientists have been able to calculate the approximate number of stars in the universe, and they have confirmed what Carl Sagan said decades ago, 'There are more stars in the universe than there are grains of sand on the Earth". Think about that for a moment. There are more stars in our universe than grains of sand on all the oceans floors, more stars than sand on all the beaches, and more stars than grains of sand in all the deserts. That is a pretty big God. And remember our universe is constantly expanding. Why would we ever put limitations on God? God that is infinite Love, infinite Knowledge, infinite Power. God is ALL. Why would we not believe that all things are possible?

Another diminution belief I have found many have, is that they place limitations on themselves. They have forgotten they are children of God. The God that created this expansive remarkable, astonishing, miraculous universe. And because they have forgotten they are created in God's image, they place restrictions on themselves. This serves no one. Limiting oneself does not serve you, others and it certainly does not serve God.

One way to help identify limiting beliefs is to ask yourself the following questions.

For your desires to transpire what must you believe both consciously and subconsciously?

_____

_____

_____

_____

_____

If what I'm wanting is not materializing then what am I thinking consciously and/or subconsciously that is getting in the way? Or simply, what limited beliefs might I have?

_____

_____

_____

_____

_____

Sometimes, we discover a belief that we don't actually think we deserve whatever it is that we want. If you truly believe that you are worthy of whatever you ask, you are opening the door for yourself to receive it. As a child of God you are incredibly deserving of all that you ever desire. No one is more deserving than you. God does not play favorites. You are just as worthy as the next person. I address in more detail how to tackle potential self-worth and self-love issues in chapter 14. Remember if it is conceivable, it is possible. I personally do not believe we are given the ability to have a true dream or desire that is not achievable. All things are possible with God.

Therefore, we may have to drop the story we've been telling ourselves, create the story we want to have, and then practice living that new story. To apply this to your own life, first choose an area of your life where you feel limited, then answer these questions.

Up to now, what have you believed was impossible in that area of your life?

_____

_____

_____

_____

_____

Now consider, how much of that is actually true?

_____

_____

_____

_____

_____

Are there any beliefs that may be untrue?

_____

_____

_____

_____

_____

I'm afraid of being wildly successful (prosperous, flourishing, healthy, thriving, having healthy loving relationships, etc.) because:

_____

_____

_____

_____

What do I get (what is my payoff) for having this limited belief? (i.e.; I'm comfortable, I don't have to put myself out there, I don't have to fear...):

_____

_____

_____

_____

_____

Now re-write your belief, turn it around into something favorable, something that brings you toward your full potential. I believe:

_____

_____

_____

_____

_____

To really master this principle we need to cultivate or **practice** the faith that what we want in our lives is actually <u>not only possible but probable</u> and to live as though it is already happening.

<u>Receive</u>

>***Psalm 37:4 (English Standard Version)***
>*Delight yourself in the LORD, and he will give you the desires of your heart.*

For some people when they hear "ask, believe and receive", sometimes the most challenging part to grasp is *receive*. Your job is to make sure you are open, ready and in a space to receive. Often you have to get out of your own way. Being open to receive means paying attention to God's responses. Don't miss the opportunity. As an example, if what you are asking for is financial security, its unlikely God is simply going to drop a suitcase of money on your doorstep. If you keep looking for the suitcase you might miss the email from a friend letting you know of an amazing job opportunity or perhaps a fantastic investment opportunity presents itself. Stay open and listen. Meditation is an extremely helpful tool in listening and I write more on that in a later chapter. Be open, listen and then you must take action.

### Matthew 7:7 (NIV)
*Ask and it will be given to you; seek and you will find; knock and the door will be opened to you.*

Ask, seek, knock, these are all actions. Too often I find folks who think they will just pray and sit back and wait for things to happen. You actually have to take action, do the work, prepare. Let me share with you the drowning man story:

A fellow was stuck on his rooftop in a flood. He was praying to God for help. Soon a man in a rowboat came by and the man shouted to the fellow on the roof, "Jump in, I can save you." The stranded fellow shouted back, "No, it's OK, I'm praying to God and he is going to save me." So the rowboat went on. Then a motorboat came by. "The man in the motorboat shouted, "Jump in, I can save you". To this the stranded fellow said, "No thanks, I'm praying to God and he is going to save me. I have faith. "So the motorboat went on. Then a helicopter came by and the pilot shouted down, "Grab this rope and I will lift you to safety." To this the stranded fellow again replied, "No thanks, I'm praying to God and he is going to save me. I have faith." So the helicopter reluctantly flew away.  Soon the water rose above the rooftop and the fellow drowned. He went to Heaven. He finally got his chance to discuss this whole situation with God, at which point he exclaimed, "I had faith in you but you didn't save me, you let me drown. I don't understand why!" To this God replied, "I sent you a rowboat and a motorboat and a helicopter, what more did you expect?" Author Unknown

By following through, doing the work, preparing, and being ready for the opportunity you are opening yourself up to receive.

You also must align yourself with your thoughts and feelings as if you already have what it is you want. Act, think, and feel as if you have already received it.  One way to do that is to give thanks in advance for the blessings you are about to receive.  Affirmative prayer is an excellent way to give thanks in advance.  We will explore more on affirmations in the next chapter.

*Once you understand that every thought you think, every word you speak, and every belief you hold is a brushstroke in the painting of your life, you begin to see the magic you bestow upon the creation of your life's masterpiece.*

Chapter Notes ~ Highlights:

_____

_____

_____

_____

_____

_____

_____

_____

_____

_____

_____

_____

_____

_____

_____

_____

_____

_____

_____

_____

_____

_____

_____

_____

# 6

## WTF? GROWING HAPPINESS

### WTF?

Oh, now, come on—that stands for "where's the focus?" not what you were thinking!

What you focus on, is what will grow. Think about it this way: you move toward what you think about. If you've ever taken a defensive-driving course, the instructor probably told you that if you hit a patch of ice or have an emergency circumstance, you should look in the direction you want to go, not where you don't want to go. You end up moving the vehicle in the direction you look.

The same holds true with your thoughts. You move your life in the direction of your thoughts. Therefore, you want to prime yourself to have thoughts that create the happy life you want.

The brain is incredibly influenced by priming. For example, if I were to say "wash" and then show you "so_p," you would likely fill in the missing letter with an *a*, creating the word "soap." On the other hand, if I said the word "eat," you would likely fill in the missing letter with a *u* to form the word "soup."

That's because our brains are fast, jumping to conclusions based on previous experiences and programming. This is due in part to the reticular activating system (RAS).

The RAS is a small part of the brain—a set of neurons and neurofibers located in the brain stem—yet it plays a vital role. It is believed to control sleep, wakefulness, behavioral motivation, and even thought to play a role in breathing and to affect the beating of the heart. It allows us the ability to focus and filter information that is let into our conscious mind.

Our brains take in incredible amounts of information every second and the RAS helps screen what parts of that information we actually need to pay attention to. We are created to filter down to what is really important and focus on it. The brain is designed to pay attention to things that keep us alive. We are also crafted to seek pleasure instead of pain. The RAS is helpful in filtering what gets through, deciding what's important.

The thing is, our thoughts help set up the parameters of what we decide is important. Try it. I want you to visualize the color red. Now, take a look around and notice how much red you see everywhere. You've told your brain that the color red is important, and now your brain really takes notice of it, even though the red was always there. Here's another example of your RAS in action: Have you ever noticed that when you decide to get a new (to you at least) vehicle that you start noticing that same make and model all over the place? There are not more vehicles of that make and model, you just told your brain to start noticing them.

### Using Affirmations and Intentions

Hence, we want to help select our thoughts—and one of the easiest ways to select our thoughts or "prime our life" is to influence our thinking using affirmations, affirmative prayer, visual reminders and intentions.

An affirmation is a statement of fact, while an intention is a resolve to act or be a certain way—in this case, to put into action your affirmation.

To create an affirmation, simply give yourself some quite space, relax, perhaps take a couple deep breaths, and then write down your goals, dreams and desires. Next put them in easy-to-repeat sentences or mantras. For example, one of the affirmations I've used while writing this book is, "I, as a joyful, grateful, passionate, best-selling author, am inspiring others to discover expanding happiness."

You'll want to design your affirmations to be positive, with passion and feeling, and also to be in the present tense (as if it is already happening). Once you have your affirmations written, you'll want to place reminders all around so that you won't forget to repeat them to yourself. (I like to use sticky notes.)

What is your goal/dream/desire?

_____

_____

_____

_____

_____

How can you state that in present tense, as if it is already happening and part of your life?

_____

_____

_____

_____

_____

How can you restate that adding emotion, passion, feeling?

_____

_____

_____

_____

_____

The best times to repeat your affirmations are in the morning upon awakening and at night before sleep, as your brain is in a more "alpha" state, allowing your subconscious to work magic.

For many, knowing what it is that they really want (what their true goals, dreams, and desires are) is the challenge. In chapter 7, I share how important having clarity

and knowing the why behind what you want is so important. Therefore you may want to revisit this section after
doing the exercises found in chapter 7.

Setting and following through with intentions is what
I consider the "action" part of affirmations. For example,
with my personal affirmation related to this book, my intentions would then follow up that statement with what I
plan to do to make my desires come true.

I use intentions to drive my life. Each morning I
set intentions for the day. Somewhat similar to tasks
or goals, intentions are more expansive. I have many
intentions to follow up my affirmations. For example, I
make an intention to find three things every day about
which to be grateful. As a result, gratitude adds to my
happiness. Since I've set gratitude as an intention, I follow through.

Many people are good at affirmations, but they fail to
put momentum behind them. That's how setting intentions helps. I like to write out my intentions for the day and
set them in a place to view often to make sure I'm on track.

Let's put this into practice for you. What one intention can
you set for your affirmation? In other words, what action
will you take?

_____

_____

_____

_____

_____

## Visual Reminders

Speaking of visual reminders, I am a huge fan of vision boards, and these, along with affirmations, are excellent tools for setting a positive tone in your life.

I have a vision board that has sections for many areas of my life—health, wealth, relationships, spirituality, my career, fun, personal growth, etc. Once a year I sit down with loads of magazines I get from friends or pick up inexpensively at the library (usually in their used-book sale section) and have fun tearing out and dreaming of all that I'd like in my world. Then I paste those images on a piece of poster board.

Now, here is the key to vision boards: you have to place them where you will see them often during the day. You want to use them to prime your mind. Therefore, you need to see them on a regular basis to remind yourself what's important.

My life has been blessed with nearly everything I've ever placed on a vision board. I encourage you to create one. Not only is it fun to create a vision board, but it's even more fun watching those images come to life. Consider having visual cues of what brings you happiness in your environment. These will be constant reminders of what you want your thoughts focused on.

## What You Resist Persists

One area of caution: be ever so watchful not to manifest things you *do not* want, simply by thinking and putting feeling—that is, emphasis—behind them.

### *Luke 21:34 (New American Standard Bible)*

*Be on guard, so that your hearts will not be weighted down with dissipation and drunkenness and the worries of life, and that day will not come on you suddenly like a trap.*

### *Proverbs 4:23 (NIV)*

*Above all else, guard your heart, for everything you do flows from it.*

Often, I find that folks focus on what they don't want in life instead of on what they *do* want. They often *ask* from a state of desperation, so they end up focusing on the absence of what they want. A key thing to remember is that the strongest picture will determine which way the brain will follow, so you want to "romance the vision." You want to spend your time and energy romancing what you want, not what you don't want.

C. G. Jung, the famous Swiss psychiatrist and psychoanalyst, said it another way: "What you resist persists."

I feel it is also significant to realize that consciously created thought is far more powerful than what I call "oops thoughts." Just because you find yourself having a thought you don't necessarily want to manifest in your life does not mean that the thought is absolutely going to transpire. As long as you don't put the energy, the belief, the feeling, the emotion, the "romance" behind it, it should just be a fleeting thought. You do want to become skilled at being able to shift those "oops thoughts" into thoughts of things you want to have come to life. Remember, you breathe life and reality into what you think and say.

I've been teaching workshops on this concept, not only for happiness but for wealth as well. I realize that how my clients handle their money mainly has to do with their "money story" (the thoughts, focus, and beliefs they hold about money).

For example, if I have clients who continually focus on debt, they generally end up staying in debt. Instead, if I have them focus on financial freedom or growth, the opposite occurs and they build wealth.

When I teach a financial workshop and ask the audience who likes the word "budget," almost nobody raises a hand, but if I ask who likes spending, almost every hand goes up. So I have the participants create spending plans instead of budgets. (It's **all** in the attitude.)

I tell my clients never to say they are broke. They are not broken. They are simply choosing not to spend their money that way at that moment. Our brains are amazingly powerful, so use your brain *for* yourself instead of *against* yourself. We were made in God's image. We can accomplish and do so much. And it's incredibly exciting that so much is within our control. Therefore, it's your job to be thinking of things you want, not things you don't want.

### Luke 6:45 (NIV)

*A good man brings good things out of the good stored up in his heart, and an evil man brings evil things out of the evil stored up in his heart. For the mouth speaks what the heart is full of.*

### Proverbs 12:25 (ESV)

*Anxiety in a man's heart weighs it down, but a good word makes it glad.*

Chapter Notes ~ Highlights:

_____

_____

_____

_____

_____

_____

_____

_____

_____

_____

_____

_____

_____

_____

_____

_____

_____

_____

_____

_____

_____

_____

_____

_____

# 7

## CLEARLY HAPPY

For many folks, one of the most challenging aspects of directing thoughts is that they either don't know what actually makes them happy or they don't know **why** they want what they want. If you don't know what it is you truly want, how will you ever get it? Imagine that you are going on a trip, to map out your journey, you need to know where you are and where it is you are going. If you don't have a destination in mind then any road will do. Determining this personal clarity is critical. We learned in chapter 5- Intentional Happiness, the significance of *ask, believe, and receive*. We discussed the incredible power of our words and thoughts, especially when we are intentional with what we say and think. Yet another very important aspect of the *ask* part of the equation is being absolutely clear on what it is you are asking God for. The clearer you are on what it is you are requesting, the more likely you will receive it.

To help with the clarity process I often have clients do the following exercises:

## Be, Do, Have, Give

Whether clients are seeing me for financial coaching, happiness coaching, or for a workshop, I have them all do the same exercise so that they can clarify what is important to them. I call it "Be, Do, Have, Give."

Here is how you do it: Get a piece of paper and draw four columns. Label the four columns "Be," "Do," "Have," and "Give." Then set a timer for one minute, and in the first column, write down everything you ever wanted to be. For example, I want to be healthy, wealthy, happy, inspiring, gracious, passionate, giving, a doctor, an author, etc. You are not allowed to judge, just write down everything that comes to mind during that minute.

After one minute, move to the "do" column. Write down everything you want to do, such as swim with the dolphins, write a book, go to Italy, Spain, Portugal, New Orleans, etc.

After that, set the timer for another minute and write down everything you want to have. For instance, I want peace, an RV, a boat, a lakefront home, love, happiness, health, happy relationships, etc.

For the final minute, write down everything you want to give. For me, that looks like this: I want to give my love, expertise, time, money, etc.

Use the space below to do this exercise, now… it's only four minutes.

| Be | Do | Have | Give |
| --- | --- | --- | --- |
| | | | |

Once you've finished the list, give yourself some time, and then go back a little while later and highlight the top four or five things on your list that makes your soul sing. Those are the areas where you want to direct your thoughts. (I want to emphasize that the "be" part of this exercise is just as important as the others. Being is just as important as doing.)

### Write the Story/Movie of You

Another exercise I often recommend for clarity is to write a short story, a movie, or a screen play about the amazing, spectacular, fabulous life of you. Remember you are the author, the director and the star of this production. This story will help you identify what's important to you and what makes you happy. It helps illuminate purpose and your calling. Before you begin, ask yourself the following questions.

If you were given a magic wand and could have any life you dreamed of; if money was not an issue, what would you do?

_____

_____

_____

_____

_____

What are you passionate about, what makes you feel alive?

_____

_____

_____

_____

_____

What is your brilliance?

_____

_____

_____

_____

_____

How are you sharing that brilliance?

_____

_____

_____

_____

Where are you adding value?

_____

_____

_____

_____

How are you making a difference?

_____

_____

_____

_____

What are your strengths and how are you using them?

_____

_____

_____

_____

_____

What life experiences do you want to have?

_____

_____

_____

_____

What do you want to achieve?

_____

_____

_____

_____

What are you in awe about or appreciate in life?

_____

_____

_____

_____

When you feel you are most happy, what makes you feel that way?

_____

_____

_____

_____

_____

What are you most proud and excited about in your life?

_____

_____

_____

_____

_____

How would you describe your purpose (calling), and how purposeful are you each day?

_____

_____

_____

_____

_____

If you could ask for help to achieve the life you've always dreamed about who/what would you ask for?

_____

_____

_____

_____

_____

What fears would you like to overcome?

_____

_____

_____

_____

_____

What do you do to feed your soul?

_____

_____

_____

_____

_____

What do you do for your health?

_____

_____

_____

_____

_____

Now that you have an understanding for what is really important to you, begin your story. Write down what you are doing, who you are with, what kind of living arrangements and environment you have, what you are feeling, what are you experiencing. What are you wearing? What is the weather like? Is the sun shining and can you feel its warmth on your skin? What do you smell? Does it smell like fresh cut grass, suntan lotion, the ocean, spring freshness, etc.? What are you doing for fun? What are you doing for work? Do you have pets, what kind, what are their names? Do you have a garden, what's in it? Are you laughing, smiling, and so on. Use such detail that you actually see and feel yourself doing and being those things. Once you have completed your story, set it aside for a period of time and go back with a highlighter and emphasize those things that resonate with you the most. Again, what in your story makes your soul sing? These exercises are designed to help you clarify what really matters to you.

My Story/Movie:

_____

_____

_____

_____

_____

_____

_____

_____

_____

_____

_____

_____

_____

_____

_____

## Folded-Paper Exercise

The folded-paper exercise is an easy task, simply take a piece of paper and fold it in half and then in half again and again and again, until you have a little two-inch rectangle. When you unfold it, there should be sixteen folded squares. In each square, write something you want to be sure is in your life. This could be a fun experience, something you want, a goal you want to achieve, a feeling, a condition, i.e.; health, peace, etc.—anything at all that you'd like in your life. Be sure to fill in all the boxes.

Then carry that with you everywhere (I keep mine in my wallet and have a copy on my desk) as a reminder of those things you want to bring into your world.

When you assess your answers and responses to these exercises, you'll want to look at the common elements. Those are the things you want to focus on, to put action behind (to write affirmations and intentions for) and to make happen.

## A Guiding Word

To further remind myself and prime my life, I like to set a word of intent; a guiding word for a year. Jon Gordon, Dan Brittan, Jimmy Page have written a book called "One Word". It is a quick 45 minute read that helps you identify your one word. For me, I ask God for guidance and then I brainstorm the top words that defined how I want to live and guide my life for the year. Words that have deep meaning for me on something I want to enhance during the year. Then I get out the old fashioned dictionary and defined them and then decide on the one that I feel best expresses my intention(s). I then put that word on my vision board, I even made some stamped metal jewelry (necklaces and bracelet that I could wear), I write it on my planner, and place it in areas of my home, work, car for a reminder of where I want my energies to focus. My word for this year is "Miracles". I want to attract, be, and live a life of miracles.

Let's discover your inspirational word for the year, the following is a guide to help you uncover your guiding word.

Brainstorm Words:

_____

_____

_____

Define your top three choices:

_____

_____

_____

_____

_____

_____

_____

_____

_____

My Word of Intent for the Year is:

_____

Now write down three things you'll do to remind yourself to live your guiding word.

_____

_____

_____

_____

_____

By using affirmations, intentions, and visualization, you are imprinting, priming, and rewiring your brain for happiness. All of these exercises will help you prioritize where to put your focus, your energies, your actions, your intentions, and your prayers.

<u>Clarifying the Why</u>

> *He who has a why to live can bear almost any how.*
> *~Friedrich Nietzsche*

Elucidating the *why*, is an essential part of the clarity process. Without understanding exactly why you want something it is challenging to achieve and manifest it. Defining the why does a couple things. First, it helps you to be sure, that what it is you are asking for, is really what you want. To discover if you really want it, you need to know the **why** you want it!

Secondly, knowing the why opens the door to the emotion behind that desire. The *why* is the passion and the reason behind the *what* and with the *why* you will find the *how*. Remember in the *ask, believe, receive* formula you have to act as if you already are receiving the blessing. In order to do that, you need to act, think, and feel as if you have already received. You need to define the why so you can fully tap into the feeling behind your desire. The *why* is the energy behind your *want*.

Answering the questions below will help you to identify your WHY:

State the Goal:

_____

_____

_____

_____

_____

Why do you want that?

_____

_____

_____

_____

_____

What does that give you?

_____

_____

_____

_____

_____

How does that make you feel?

_____

_____

_____

_____

_____

Once you know your *why,* the how will present itself!

Here's an example:

State the Goal: Write a book on Happiness and God

Why do I want that? Because more and more people are moving away from God/Faith/Belief of a Higher Power. And because, without belief in something bigger than yourself, then when unfortunate life events happen (and they will), people are thrown into the pits of despair. Because my heart breaks at the rampant depression and suicide rate. And because, I feel if more people were reminded that there is a God (a higher power) and that we are biologically designed to be happy; and if I could share the science behind happiness/wellbeing and what a difference each of us can make in our own level of happiness, then maybe, just maybe, life could be a little easier, a little happier, a little more full of Love. Because with a belief in something greater than oneself, you have hope, and with hope all things are possible.

What does that give me? It inspires me, and gives me a sense of faith, hope encouragement and of empowerment.

How does that make me feel? It makes me feel as if I can help make a difference. It gives me a purpose in life, it inspires me to be the best person I can be, it makes me feel hopeful, it's how I can share Love, and it makes me feel happy!

And that my friends, is the why behind this book. And with the why, there is no stopping me. With the why, I created my happiness workshops and share them as often as possible with others. With the *why*, it gives me the energy, the passion, the courage. With the *why* **you** are now reading this book. I don't have to know the how I just keep at it, I prepare, I work and I let go and let God take care of the rest.

Declutter Your Life, Declutter Your Mind
A last tip on clarity…Lighten your load.

If you start decluttering your space and releasing resentments, clearing out thoughts and things that no longer serve you, you allow room for what you really want in life. By cleaning out and decluttering, you permit space for the ALL your life can be, it is so freeing and brings such lightness.

My favorite way to start is to pick a small area—say a drawer—and just commit to cleaning that one area out. Then add another small space, and then another, etc.

Or commit to five minutes of decluttering. I set the timer on my phone and start at it. When the timer goes off, I'm done. I get such a feeling of satisfaction. Just make the commitment and do it. Then sit back and notice the flow, the peace, the calm.

What one area can you commit to decluttering this week?

_____

_____

_____

_____

_____

Chapter Notes ~ Highlights:

_____

_____

_____

_____

_____

_____

_____

_____

_____

_____

_____

_____

_____

_____

_____

_____

_____

_____

_____

_____

_____

_____

_____

_____

# 8

# THE MAGIC OF HAPPINESS

Now you know that the purpose of life is to be happy, as God designed us for happiness, and that your thoughts create that happiness. You also have learned how to create intentional happiness, that what you focus on grows, and that you should prime your life. BUT...

How do you tell your brain what to think about while you are in the midst of a tragic situation, a crisis, or a stressful moment? Here is where a great deal of the **magic** of designing a happy life exists.

> *Between stimulus and response there is a space. In that space is our power to choose our response. In our response lies our growth and our freedom.*
>
> —*Viktor E. Frankl*

I could not agree more. I'd also add that mastering the space is where a considerable amount of your happiness lies. So how do you do that?

You want to exercise and train your brain to pause before you immediately respond. To have an opportunity to choose what thoughts you want to run with.

Why do you have to learn to pause? Because if you don't, your brain will hijack you.

You see, we have these fast brains. As I mentioned earlier, our brains are designed to keep us alive and move us toward pleasure and away from pain.

Let me give you an example of how our fast brain works: Imagine you are hiking and on the ground you see a curled-up object. Your brain will naturally have you proceed with caution or—probably more likely—have you jump back. Why? Because we are wired to avoid threatening circumstances.

We have a built-in survival system that has us fight, flee, or freeze in the midst of danger. So we see what we perceive to be a snake, and our bodies automatically respond to the coiled-up object by releasing a chemical that gets our hearts pumping so we can run. When we realize the bent object was not a snake at all, but just a stick, it still takes a few moments for our bodies to settle back down because our brain released chemicals to activate our flight response. This is how we are wired.

However, when it comes to our happiness, you want to learn to slow down your fast brain, to exercise the pause in between stimulus and response. That way, you can have the opportunity to choose which thought you want to go with instead of having your brain dictate how you perceive things.

### James 1:19 (ESV)
*Know this, my beloved brothers: let every person be quick to hear, slow to speak, slow to anger.*

Remember that it's our thoughts that create our emotions, which create our perceptions, which create our beliefs, which create our responses and behaviors, which affect things like our relationships and ultimately shapes our entire life. **Therefore, the secret to sustained happiness is to learn to expand the space (create a pause) between stimulus and response so that you can decide how you want to respond instead of having your fast brain decide for you.**

You have over 60,000 thoughts per day, and most of those are the same thoughts you had yesterday. If you want to change your life, you need to change your thoughts. In order to do that, you need to learn how to create a pause, in order to allow yourself time to decide what you want to think.

Remember, the brain has this amazing ability to do some awesome editing. It then presents an immediate response due to all your years of programming and your RAS. As a result, you view that response as reality, the only truth. In fact, though, that was only one option or way of seeing the world out of literally tens of thousands of choices.

Let's review the science behind all this. As we discussed in previous chapters, our brain is changeable; it's plastic. Thus we can actually retrain our brain to respond differently. We can program it to pause between the immediate situation (the stimulus) and our response. Then we can decide which response we want instead of going with the first edited choice presented by our fast brain.

How do we do that? We slow down our fast brains so we can create the space to choose. We exercise and strengthen the ability to pause between stimulus and response, and we allow ourselves to see several ways of looking at the situation and deciding carefully which choice we want to feel and which way we want to lean.

One way I do that, when faced with a provoking or challenging situation, is by asking myself, "Is this worth losing my cool over?" Sometimes it is, and I'll let myself have a freak-out moment. And then I just as easily decide, "OK, done with that. Now how do I want to feel?"

Let me give you an example. I was recently traveling and going through airport security. I was informed by one of the TSA officers that I'd need to check my bag. I was perplexed and explained that the bag was regulation size. I was told I would not be allowed to go farther in line until I had checked the bag. I asked if I could check the bag after I got through security and was told no. So I checked the bag and proceeded through security.

I placed my purse on the conveyor belt, took off my shoes, placed them on the belt as well, went through the scan machine and then waited on the other side of the scan for my things. Then I saw the dreaded belt reversal. You know, when they are taking another look at the X-Ray image. Sure enough the TSA officer asked who the purse belonged to and asked me to follow her. I grabbed my shoes and went to the designated area. I was told I had something that looked like a horseshoe in my purse. I did indeed have a small horseshoe that was given to me as a gift at a wedding I had attended the day before. I went to get the horseshoe out to show her. She literally slapped my hand back telling me not to touch the bag.

*She* pulled it out and informed me that I could not take it on the plane with me as it could be used as a weapon and that I'd have to check it. Well, I would have checked it if they had not insisted I check my suitcase already.

So, at that moment, I literally asked myself if this was worth getting upset over and you know what? I decided that it was. I asked to speak to a supervisor, who proceeded to tell me that the small horseshoe could be used as "brass knuckles". I was stunned as he actually subsequently put the horseshoe around two of his knuckles to demonstrate.

I said some choice words about how ridiculous it was. My husband was surprised to see me "lose it", as he has rarely seen me get upset (at least not in public -*wink*). He put his arm around me, worried that I might be escalating the situation, which might not end well for me.

At that moment, I decided I was done feeling angry and frustrated. I was not going to let this affect the rest of my trip. I made a conscious choice about how I wanted to feel, and I changed my feelings.

*The magic lies in the pause and realizing you can change how you are feeling at any moment, even while in the midst of a situation.*

MFI

And how do you create the pause? You need to craft and master "interrupter skills."

What do I mean by that? You need to be able to purposely construct an interruption to stop the current thought flow and ultimate reaction so that you have the ability to have another thought—any other thought.

If you do not pause, you will continue to feed your current thoughts, emotions, and feelings. And more and more chemicals to match those thoughts will be dumped into your body, which will create even more feelings and thoughts and more chemicals.

So next time, when your mind is doing a number on you (my friend David calls it a mind freak-out or more bluntly a mindfu@k), how do you interrupt your brain so you can even entertain a new thought? I believe that is a key element to sustained happiness. So I have developed several MFI ("mind freak-out interruption") skills.

When in a situation with another person, one of my favorite MFI skills is to remind myself that I am the author, star, and director of the Christine show and to ask myself how I want my star actress to respond in that moment. How do I want this happy ending to happen? How would my highest self respond? And then I can shift. Sometimes, I actually say "plot twist" out loud and choose a new scene.

When my mind is simply playing over and over a situation and continually feeding a response that results in a feeling I don't want, I seek to interrupt that cycle. I may just need a distraction from the situation, so I get up and go for a walk, see a movie, pick up a book, or call a friend. (If YOU do this, remember: don't talk about what you don't want.) Other times, I imagine I have a large "pause" button in my brain that I can push at any time.

Do anything to stop the negative, unwanted self-talk or thoughts so that you can allow another possibility to be entertained.

One of my coaches, Leslie, taught me to smell the number nine. Try it: smell the number nine. What does it smell like? In attempting to "smell the number," you take your brain off the current way of thinking and move your mental activity into the frontal lobe, which creates an interruption.

I also use "what if" to generate possibilities (discussed in more detail in chapter 16). What if this is not the only possibility? What are other ways of looking at this?

For example, there are a lot of changes occurring within the financial industry right now—legislatively, with many products, with how we are being told we can help our clients. Some appear to be helpful and some not so much, and many of my peers and co-advisors are panicking and thinking the worst. They are thinking of leaving the business (flight). Or they are becoming angry and bitter (fight) because they feel that their business will be devastated and that their clients will be hurt by the changes. Some are doing nothing (frozen) in fear of what could happen.

I have chosen to view the situation with a "what if." What if this is the best thing that could happen for my clients and for me? I'm still able to go about my business and help my clients in the best way possible instead of giving up like many of my coworkers.

Why worry about something when you have no idea what the outcome will be? So many people worry about things that never end up happening. Worrying doesn't change the outcome; it just steals your joy. Instead of worrying about what can go wrong, I try to shift and get excited about what could go right. Remember to use the "what if" for an outcome you'd **prefer**, not for what you don't want.

### Philippians 4:6–7 (ESV)

*Do not be anxious about anything, but in everything by prayer and supplication with thanksgiving let your requests be made known to God. And the peace of God, which surpasses all understanding, will guard your hearts and your minds in Christ Jesus.*

### Matthew 6:27 (New Living Translation)

*Can all your worries add a single moment to your life?*

### 1 Peter 5:7 (International Standard Version)

*Throw all your worry on him, because he cares for you.*

Yet another fabulous interrupter skill is what psychologist's call, "name it to tame it". I like to expand on that and instead of naming it, try to describe your interpretation or perception of what is happening using only sensational words. For example: instead of saying "I'm Angry", I might say, "my hands got sweaty, my heart was pumping, my skin was tingling, and I felt warm". This moves you from the creation center of your brain—expanding those thoughts and emotions —to your frontal lobe, which creates an interruption of the neurotransmitter chemicals that are causing your unwanted feelings. This allows an interruption so that you can entertain another thought. When presenting my happiness workshop, I'll often have the participants practice this with a partner. I have them wear blindfolds and pull an object out of a bag; then they have to describe that object to their partners only using sensational words. This helps them practice creating the pause.

Examples of Sensational Words:
airy, bloated, blocked, breathless, bright, brisk, brittle, bubbly, burning, buzzy, calm, centered, clammy, clearheaded, clenched, cold, cool, congested, constricted, contracted, damp, dark, deflated, dense, disconnected, dizzy, draining, dry, dull, electric, empty, energized, expanded, expansive, faint, flaccid, flowing, fluid, flushed, fluttery, fragile, frantic, frowning, frozen, full, fuzzy, grounded, having butterflies, heavy, heated, hollow, hot, icy, inflated, itchy, jagged, jarring, jittery, jumpy, knotted, light, lighthearted, loose, luminous, moist, nervous, nervy, numb, open, painful, paralyzed, pounding, pressurized, prickly, puffy, pulsing, queasy, quivery, racing, radiating, ragged, raw, referring, relaxed, releasing, restricted, shaky, sharp, shivery, skippy, smiley, smooth, spacey, spacious, spinning, still, streaming, stringy, strong, suffocating, sweaty, tense, thick, thin, throbbing, tight,

tingly, trembling, tremulous, twitchy, uncomfortable, warm, wavy (having waves of energy), wobbly, wooden, whooshing

Prayer is an incredible MFI! Taking time to pause and say a quick prayer may be just the space you need to allow yourself the opportunity to have another way to look at the situation.

### Jeremiah 33:3(ESV)
*Call to me and I will answer you, and will tell you great and hidden things that you have not known.*

### Romans 12:12 (NIV)
*Be joyful in hope, patient in affliction, faithful in prayer.*

Emotional Freedom Technique (EFT), a form of psychological acupressure practiced by tapping on the energy meridians on your head, chest, and hands and voicing positive affirmations, is an extremely effective MFI and also helps with restoring emotional balance.

And finally, my absolutely favorite MFI is to use a visualization tool that my friend David shared with me. When I'm going through a tough situation, I imagine that God has me in a large slingshot and He is pulling back (that's the yuck I'm feeling, the transition, the challenge, the change) but soon He is going to release and catapult me into amazing things. Too often we tend to jump out of the slingshot while it's being pulled back, right before the miracles manifest.

You need to learn to hang in there, be patient, and then be ready for the ride of your life as you are soon to be propelled into all that you desire.

Chapter Notes ~ Highlights:

_____

_____

_____

_____

_____

_____

_____

_____

_____

_____

_____

_____

_____

_____

_____

_____

_____

_____

_____

_____

_____

_____

_____

_____

_____

_____

# 9

# SHOPPING FOR HAPPINESS

So now, you've mastered the pause. You've created and are practicing your own interrupter skills. Now what? How do you choose another thought?

This is the easy part: you get to go shopping! Shop for how you want to feel. Shop! Woohoo! Shop to your heart's content! Shop, shop, and shop some more!! It's the best shopping ever, because you are shopping for happiness.

Creating the interruption allows you space for another thought or way of looking at things. You now have the ability to ask yourself, "Is there any other way to look at this? How could this be useful? Are the things I am telling myself true? Is there another way to interpret this? How can this be useful? What else could this mean? What can I learn from this?" When you can change your perceptions you can change your life.

Perception is active not passive. YOU control your thoughts. You get to choose how you want to look at any situation. Remember, situations do not have inherent meaning. You assign a situation meaning based on your fast brain. Past experiences, values, and beliefs about yourself and others determine how you interpret the event. When you shop for happiness you allow yourself the ability to choose another way to look at the situation, to see things differently and to lean into how you want to feel about it. You get to choose how you view it and pick what serves you, what feels good. In coaching we call this ability to shop for happiness- **reframing**. When you can shift how you look at things you can shift your experience of it.

Give yourself at least four or five other ways of looking at it before choosing. Often I suggest throwing out the first and second thought and continuing to come up with alternative options until you find one that moves you in the direction you want.

I'm not talking window shopping here. I want you to actually try the thought on, see how comfortable it is. You know, when you go shopping for a new pair of jeans, you most likely don't buy the first pair you see. If you are like me, you take a dozen pairs into the dressing room. You put them on, and you see if they stretch and move with you, if they're comfortable, if they're a good match for your body type. You try on pair after pair until you find the one that fits just right.

Well, I want you to do the same for your thoughts. Try them on. Do they feel good? Do they make you feel expansive, light, better? Or are they tight, constrictive, and limiting? You'll most often find that you want to lean into the good.

Keep in mind that all of life is energy, and that energy is expansive. If you want more joy and happiness in your life, you need to lean into that energy. I will most often chose to lean into the good—not always, mind you, but most often.

So give yourself a chance to shop for how you truly want to feel. Consider using the following chapter notes section to reframe a situation in your life. Write down four or five alternative ways to look at it, then pick the one that feels the best.

***Remember, it is never the thing, it is always what you think about the thing!***

If you'd like to hear more about WTF? (Where's The Focus), how to expand the pause by using interrupters (MFIs- Mind Freak-out Interrupters), and Shopping for Happiness (reframing), check out the TEDx talk I did called "WTF?- Pausing to Grow Happiness" available on YouTube.

Chapter Notes ~ Highlights:

# 10

## DESIGNED FOR HAPPINESS

You are whole, complete, and perfect just as you are. And being whole, complete, and perfect, you are enough, just as you are. **YOU ARE ENOUGH!**

This is **not** about staying positive all the time. Being human means living and experiencing a wide range of emotions and thoughts. Sometimes, you are going to feel angry, frustrated, sad, scared, upset, etc. There is nothing wrong with that. That is being human, and it doesn't make you a negative person. All emotions have value. Think about it for a moment, take anger for example: Anger cues you to pay attention, it motivates you to take action. Sadness, is cathartic, cleansing, releasing. We have the ability to feel all emotions because they all matter and serve a purpose in our lives.

Sometimes life throws things at us that are tragic, sad, and extremely challenging. We don't need to sugarcoat those things. We are designed to experience the full variety of emotions. The key to lasting happiness is realizing that you actually have choices. Although we may be sad or angry about something temporarily (I personally never want to *stay* there), we also need to realize we can move on to another feeling when we decide. As they say, "You can pull over; just don't park or move in." Life is full of necessary stops, but they are not our destinations. I believe, it was Lisa Nichols, who said, "Don't put a period in your story, where God put a comma."

Remember in chapter 8 when I shared my airport story? In that moment I chose to be upset at first—and then I chose not to let the situation ruin my trip. I was able to shift my thoughts and make a choice. This is because I have learned to make happiness a practice. I have fortified that area in my brain to be able to shift and choose.

This choice was once explained to me as a "life buffet." At a buffet, you have many choices of what you can put on your plate—beef, chicken, fish. Let's say you want beef. You don't sit there and argue with the chef over why he has fish out. You simply choose not to have the fish.

The same scenario applies with emotions. They're all available for a full depth of human experiences, none necessarily right or wrong. Some people have fish, some have beef. You get to choose what you want on your plate. Even in the worst of situations, you still have choices.

Of course, most often you will not go from sad to happy instantaneously (and you probably wouldn't want to). In an upsetting or tragic situation, you want to experience sadness until it no longer serves you. When you are ready to move on, try the next best thought or feeling, and try to hold that. That next best feeling might actually be anger. And when you're done with that, you might move on to, say, surprise, and then, possibly, acceptance, and then, perhaps, hope, moving your emotions forward.

Try each one on for a while and see how it feels. Keep trying emotions until you find one that moves you in the direction you want to go. The more you practice this, the faster you can move through.

Realizing that it's OK to stay sad as long as you want to or feel you need to is freeing. Understanding that it is within your control—that how you feel is up to you—is empowering. Recognizing that God created you whole, complete, and perfect, that you are ultimately designed for happiness, and that you have the full range of humanity available at any time so that you get to experience any emotion you need or want to is awe inspiring.

William James said that the greatest weapon against stress is the ability to choose one thought over another.

### Psalm 139:14 (God's Word)

*I will give thanks to you because I have been so amazingly and miraculously made. Your works are miraculous, and my soul is fully aware of this.*

Chapter Notes ~ Highlights:

_____

_____

_____

_____

_____

_____

_____

_____

_____

_____

_____

_____

_____

_____

_____

_____

_____

_____

_____

_____

_____

_____

_____

_____

_____

_____

_____

# 11

## HAPPILY MINDFUL

Want to see miracles manifest and multiply in your life? Then simply add meditation to your daily practice.

We talk to God through prayer. We humans tend to be great at talking yet not so great at listening. That is what meditation is (for me, at least): it's listening. You will recall, when I shared about *receive*, in *ask, believe and receive*, how important it is to be open, to listen for God's responses, I do that with Meditation.

We need to slow down the brain chatter so we can hear God's answers. We have to pause for the divine response. Meditation strengthens and builds the ability to create and expand the "pause" and it allows for clarity.

There are many books available on mindfulness and the power, peace, and clarity it brings to folks. So, I'm not going to elaborate on the how, when, where, what type, etc. of meditation much here. However, if you don't already have a meditation practice, I am going to highly recommend you start, even if you only start out with a couple minutes of mindful reflection a day, you'll notice the profound results. There are so many types and forms of meditation. Experiment and find the ones that resonate with you. I personally vary the type of mindfulness I do, from guided meditation, to walking meditation, and everything in between. I like to mix it up.

An example, of a really easy starting meditation I often use, is what I call the Peace Meditation —I believe it was originally introduced by Gabrielle Bernstein:

Start by setting a timer for two minutes. Simply sit in a comfortable position and touch your thumb to your index finger and say "peace," then move your thumb to touch your middle finger and say "begins," then move your thumb to touch your ring finger and say "with," and finally move your thumb to touch your ring finger and say "me."

"Peace begins with me. Peace begins with me."

Repeat this several times for two minutes. Then increase your time from two minutes daily for one week to three minutes daily the next week, and so on.

Meditation literally results in miracles. Meditation is also one of the greatest manifestation tools that I use to bring what I want into my world. Mindfulness allows me to open up to God. It allows me to hone my skill set of creating space and pause. It allows my brain a chance to "reboot."

In our office, anytime we have trouble with an electronic device, our first response to resolve the issue is to unplug it. Once we plug it back in, it often works. That is how I see meditation for your brain. It reboots the system.

### Psalm 49:3 (NIV)
*My mouth will speak words of wisdom; the meditation of my heart will give you understanding.*

### Psalm 19:14 (ESV)
*Let the words of my mouth and the meditation of my heart be acceptable in your sight, O LORD, my rock.*

Need more reasons to start meditating? It's been shown that mindfulness increases focus and concentration and reduces stress. It is known to improve empathy and decrease impulsiveness.

Biologically speaking, meditation can decrease negative inflammatory activity, increase positive antiviral response, slow aging, improve cardiovascular health, improve the function of specific strains of immune cells, increase antibody production, and even alter our genetic makeup. Meditation has also been proven to increase happiness!

Chapter Notes ~ Highlights:

# 12

## THE HAPPINESS
## CONNECTION

Next to carefully selecting our thoughts and words, having loving relationships has the single most substantial impact on your happiness level. The quality of your relationships with God, friends, family, coworkers, neighbors, and others is tightly related to your well-being and personal happiness.

You want to spend time developing close relationships and making your important relationships in life a priority. Unfortunately, when we are not intentional about relationships, those friendships will inadvertently take a back seat to other priorities. We know that one of the greatest regrets people express in the final moments of their life, is having worked too hard and not taken time for the most meaningful parts of life…friendships, family, and doing things that make themselves truly happy. While maintaining and developing new relationships takes time and energy, the lasting joy and comfort makes the investment worthwhile.

Quality counts more than quantity, so you want to choose, nurture, and cultivate close relationships. When choosing those friends, be discerning and select carefully. Surround yourself with folks who lift you up, encourage you, add value, help you grow, and give you energy—not those who continually zap you or tear you down. God further guides us and advises us to be watchful of whom we spend our time with:

### Proverbs 13:20 (ESV)
*Whoever walks with the wise becomes wise, but the companion of fools will suffer harm.*

### Proverbs 22:24–25 (ESV)
*Make no friendship with a man given to anger, nor go with a wrathful man, lest you learn his ways and entangle yourself in a snare.*

### 1 Corinthians 15:33 (NIV)
*Do not be misled: "Bad company corrupts good character."*

We want to spend time developing loving, caring relationships not only because they make us happier; social connections make us healthier too. Friendships are good for both your mental and physical health. When you have healthy connections, you are less likely to experience anxiety, sadness, depression, low self-esteem, problems with loneliness, and eating, sleeping, drug, and drinking issues. Healthy connections increase your sense of belonging and purpose, improve self-worth, and helps you cope.

Sustaining meaningful relationships can be as beneficial to our health as proper diet, exercise, and adequate sleep. Scientist have long been researching the close biological and behavioral benefits of social connections. They have found that strong relationships help relieve harmful levels of stress, and stress can adversely affect your digestive function, immune system, and coronary function.

### *Having quality relationships matters!*

New research is even suggesting that addiction is closely related to the lack of connection. Keep in mind that many of us (whether you like to admit it or not) often have some degree of trouble with addiction. We are an addicted society, whether our addiction is to food, alcohol, spending, sex, video games, smoking, shopping, electronics, or risk taking. Pretty much anything that is out of balance is usually an addiction.

So take time to develop friendships and relationships and to harvest the joy in your connections as they add to a happy and healthy life!

Happy Chat

Since quality relationships have such a vital impact on our happiness and health, taking the time to learn and develop healthy communication and relationship-building skills will help nourish and enrich friendships.

One of the most profound relationship-building skills I ever learned was to take 100 percent responsibility in the relationship. We've often been taught that a fifty-fifty relationship is what we should strive for. We tend to spend a great deal of time in a relationship proving we are right. *However, when you and your partner each take 100 percent responsibility, the relationship thrives.*

Learning to listen properly is essential to effective communication. When you learn to listen to **understand** and not just to respond, you enrich comprehension and as a result, enhance communication.

What we say and when and how we say it (that is, our tone and body language) are all fundamental to successful connections. Even during the most heated disagreements, always remember that you love and honor the person you are arguing with; you may not like the person very much at that moment, but you do love him. You now know how powerful words are, how they create your world—so use them for the good of building people up, not for tearing them down.

Let me share with you an example of how easily communication can be misunderstood and a simple fix for such cases. I've been married over thirty-four years, and one thing I know for sure is that my husband and I interpret things differently. Therefore, I've learned to be direct in my statements. For example, in the past, when I would say to him, "It would be nice if…"—thinking I've made a request—he actually has no clue that's what I've done.

What he hears is that I think something is nice. In the meantime, I'm getting more and more frustrated because the "thing" is not being done. I may even say it again and again. "It sure would be nice if..." — after several attempts I may finally burst out in irritation and say something in anger. At which time, he is genuinely surprised. It never even occurred to him I was making a request. So, I've since learned to develop the relationship skill to be specific. Instead, now I say, "I have a request; could we please _____?" And I wait for a response to be sure he heard it as a request, not a comment. This has saved us so many quarrels. It really pays off in a relationship, and actually life in general to become proficient in salubrious communication and relationship-building skills.

As with everything else I've discussed in this book thus far, the Bible perfectly exemplifies the importance of gentle communication and how harsh language is a communication killer. Here are a few of my favorites/the most poignant examples...

### Ephesians 4:29 (ESV)

*Let no corrupting talk come out of your mouths, but only such as is good for building up, as fits the occasion, that it may give grace to those who hear.*

### Psalm 141:3 (ESV)

*Set a guard, O LORD, over my mouth; keep watch over the door of my lips!*

### Proverbs 15:2 (ESV)

*The tongue of the wise commends knowledge, but the mouths of fools pour out folly.*

### 2 Timothy 2:16 (ESV)

*But avoid irreverent babble, for it will lead people into more and more ungodliness.*

### Proverbs 12:18 (ESV)

*There is one whose rash words are like sword thrusts, but the tongue of the wise brings healing.*

### Proverbs 16:23 (ESV)

*The heart of the wise makes his speech judicious and adds persuasiveness to his lips.*

### Proverbs 18:2 (ESV)

*A fool takes no pleasure in understanding, but only in expressing his opinion.*

### Proverbs 18:17 (ESV)

*The one who states his case first seems right, until the other comes and examines him.*

### Proverbs 18:13 (ESV)

*If one gives an answer before he hears, it is his folly and shame.*

### Proverbs 29:20 (ESV)

*Do you see a man who is hasty in his words? There is more hope for a fool than for him.*

### 1 Thessalonians 5:11 (ESV)

*Therefore encourage one another and build one another up, just as you are doing.*

Chapter Notes ~ Highlights:

# 13

## PEACEFULLY HAPPY

Since we are created in God's image, and God is Love, we are also Love. We are all energetic beings. The more we can love, the higher our energy and vibration are. When you hold onto hate and anger, these feelings lower your vibration.

You have to care more about your happiness than about holding on to that anger. Would you rather be happy or right? Would you rather have peace in your heart or bitterness? Holding on to hate and anger is like drinking poison to spite someone else. It doesn't work; only you get injured in the process.

As odd as it may seem, I once found it easier to forgive strangers than myself or my close family members or friends. Then I was blessed to have a coach who suggested that all are innocent. She said she couldn't imagine that people would choose to make poor decisions or mistakes. She suggested that when people know better, they usually do better, **and just because I think they should know better doesn't mean they do**. Until they know better, they are to be viewed as innocent. If I see other people as proceeding from a state of innocence, this perception allows me to drop judgment and to forgive easily. I practice forgiveness for the sake of *my* health and happiness. And that forgiveness practice begins with forgiving myself.

## AFGO

Speaking of mistakes, I, like everyone else on this planet, make plenty of them. One of my favorite ways of shifting from berating myself over a gaffe to embracing forgiveness is to remind myself that this is just another growth opportunity. I actually use the acronym AFGO: Another Fabulous Growth Opportunity.

To be honest, sometimes I use a word other than "fabulous" that also starts with $F$ and ends in *ing* (I'm far from perfect). It makes me laugh, which is an amazing interrupter skill; then I ask, "What can I learn from this? How can I grow?"

I read something recently, and I don't know who wrote it, but I found it profound: "Being continually angry is punishing ourselves for another's mistake." Isn't that true? I also like another analogy: holding on to anger is like being under a severe storm cloud, and as that cloud moves, you follow it everywhere it goes.

Ho'oponopono

Ho'oponopono is an ancient Hawaiian forgiveness and reconciliation ritual and is often translated "to make right". Many islanders believe that if you hold onto anger you invite sickness in and by practicing Ho'oponopono you can correct and restore the balance. I have experienced profound healing, clearing and peace from practicing Ho'oponopono and simply by using the mantra "I love you, I'm sorry, please forgive me, and thank you". Ho'oponopono begins with taking 100% responsibility for your life. It is your responsibility because it is your creation. The mantra, as I see it, is a prayer to God to correct internal conflict.

Four simple steps to practicing Ho'oponopono; Love, Repentance, Forgiveness and Gratitude.

Step 1. Say, "I love you". Love to yourself, Love to others, Love to God. Mean it, believe it, and proclaim it!

Step 2. Say, "I'm Sorry". For anything and everything that brings suffering to you and/or others.

Step 3. Say, "Please Forgive Me". Say it over and over and really mean it. Take responsibility and ask for forgiveness.

Step 4. Say, "Thank you". Thank yourself, thank God, and thank everyone.

I use Ho'oponopono as a prayer and meditation on a regular basis. I also use it anytime I have conflict or a struggle in my life. I've used Ho'oponopono generally as described above and I've used it specifically for particular struggles or discard, imagining the incident, individual or myself as I practice. I literally have done this practice, and had the person I've been visualizing and saying the prayer about call me within hours, saying how sorry *they* are or offering an olive branch. When used on myself, I've noticed personal issues resolve within minutes. It is so incredible to see this in action. Give it a try and be prepared to experience a profound shift in your life.

### Matthew 5:43–44 (NIV)

*You have heard that it was said,*
*"Love your neighbor and hate your enemy."*
*But I tell you: Love your enemies and pray for those*
*who persecute you.*

### 1 Peter 3:9–11 (NIV)

*Do not repay evil with evil or insult with insult. On*
*the contrary, repay evil with blessing, because to this*
*you were called so that you may inherit a blessing.*
*For,*
*"Whoever would love life*
*    and see good days*
*must keep their tongue from evil*
*    and their lips from deceitful speech.*
*They must turn from evil and do good;*
*    they must seek peace and pursue it.*

### Ephesians 4:31–32 (ESV)

*Let all bitterness and wrath and anger and clamor and slander be put away from you, along with all malice. Be kind to one another, tenderhearted, forgiving one another, as God in Christ forgave you.*

### 1 Thessalonians 5:15 (NIV)

*Make sure that nobody pays back wrong for wrong, but always strive to do what is good for each other and for everyone else.*

### Psalm 37:37 (NIV)

*Consider the blameless, observe the upright; a future awaits who seek peace.*

### 2 Corinthians 13:11 (NIV)

*Finally, brothers and sisters, rejoice! Strive for full restoration, encourage one another, be of one mind, live in peace. And the God of love and peace will be with you.*

Chapter Notes ~ Highlights:

_____

_____

_____

_____

_____

_____

_____

_____

_____

_____

_____

_____

_____

_____

_____

_____

_____

_____

_____

_____

_____

_____

_____

_____

_____

_____

_____

# 14

## THE BIOLOGY OF HAPPINESS

As previously illuminated, more and more research is being done on the biological connection between our happiness and our bodies. Happiness has been scientifically shown to refashion our cellular composition in positive ways. Our mind and immune system are intrinsically linked, and our body is a literal product of that environment. We now have a very basic understanding of this link through our understanding of neuroplasticity, epigenetics, and how our reticular activating system works. Let's look a little further into the biology of happiness.

### Happy Hormones
Feelings of happiness are correlated to the secretion of hormones and neurotransmitters in the endocrine system and

brain. Neurotransmitters are the chemical messengers that allow signals to pass the synapses cleft and transmit information from a nerve cell or neuron to a target cell (associated with the nervous system). Neurotransmitters direct behavior by stimulating an action or inhibiting an impulse. Hormones stimulate, regulate, and control the function of various tissues and organs (associated with the endocrine system). Hormones are the chemical messengers of the endocrine system and are moved by blood to target cells. **Basically, this means that neurotransmitters and hormones directly influence the emotions we feel.**

The brain and endocrine system produces hundreds of these chemicals, including dopamine, serotonin, oxytocin, and endorphins. As a result, we can literally create happiness by making our body produce more of these "feel-good" substances. Here's a snapshot of just a few of those chemicals and how you can naturally produce more.

## Create a Dopamine Drip

*Dopamine* is linked to the rewards system in the brain. It is often referred to as the "motivation hormone." It boosts focus, concentration, and drive. It's the "I can do it" center. Dopamine also makes you feel energized, upbeat, and alert. Low dopamine can lead to "the blues/blahs."

One of the ways to increase dopamine is to simply set a goal and achieve it. Consider breaking larger goals into smaller "mini" goals so you can boost your dopamine by accomplishing each of the mini-tasks.

One of my favorite things to do is make lists and mark things off the list that I have finished. Sometimes, I'll even add something that I already completed, just to be able to mark it off. This way, I've created a dopamine drip.

In chapter 7, I mentioned how good decluttering can feel. It's a fabulous dopamine enhancing exercise.

Acknowledging achievements with a hearty "Ta-dah!" also helps boost dopamine. Actually it's very important that you take time to celebrate your accomplishments so your brain sees that as a reward and motivates you more. We live in a society that sometimes puts too much emphasis on doing and we go from goal to goal without really celebrating our achievements, which often results in a feelings of overwhelm instead of joy.

Exercising and listening to your favorite song will also give you a hit of it, and meditation has been recognized to raise dopamine, which in turn increases concentration, focus, and drive (just another reason to add a daily meditation practice). Even having a favorite hobby creates a dopamine drip.

Swell Your Serotonin

*Serotonin* helps elevate mood and aids in many important functions, such as sleep, appetite, confidence, self-esteem, increased worthiness, and feelings of belonging.

Having low serotonin can create feelings of irritability, negativity, and low mood.

There are many ways to naturally increase serotonin production in your brain.

Setting and achieving goals, not only helps with dopamine production, but also helps boost serotonin.

Direct exposure to natural light, vitamin D, exercise, massage, healthy diet, and eating chocolate all intensify serotonin levels.

You also, get an incredible swell in serotonin levels by reliving or reflecting on happy or significant moments in your life.

## Elevate Your Endorphins

*Endorphins* are considered the pain-killing chemicals. They help alleviate depression and anxiety while expanding enjoyment, contentment, and euphoric feelings.

When endorphin levels are low, we can be sensitive to physical pain and can often feel sad easily.

Exercise is an excellent way to create more endorphins. Regular runners and exercisers can tell you exactly how beneficial physical activity can be because they often have what is called the "runner's high" after working out.

Laughter is also an endorphin releaser. Additionally, aromatherapy, particularly the scents of vanilla and lavender, has been linked to increased production of endorphins. Chocolate and spicy foods help stimulate production as well, and many people believe that sunlight, deep breathing, massage, acupuncture, and acupressure also boost the release of endorphins.

## Overflow your Oxytocin

*Oxytocin* creates feelings of bonding and trust, which are crucial for intimacy and healthy relationships. It has been shown to increase relaxation, lower stress and anxiety, and even lower blood pressure.

Oxytocin is naturally released during orgasms and breastfeeding and is often referred to as the "cuddle hormone."

Giving and receiving hugs, expressing your love, giving and receiving gifts, and making strong social connections are some of the best ways to naturally release oxytocin.

A favorite bonding exercise that I learned to do with my husband that greatly enhances oxytocin flow, is to place my hand on his heart and his hand on my heart, and then take my free hand and cover his hand, and his free hand over mine. Next, we simply try to match our breathing patterns and look each other in the eyes for a couple minutes. The oxytocin just pours into us and we feel incredibly connected.

## Dosing on Happiness

So if you want to get a mega dose of happiness chemicals, consider going out for a walk in the sunshine while listening to your favorite song, reveling in your recent accomplishments, coming back home and enjoying some chocolate (perhaps one of the new chili dark chocolate bars—for the spicy part), and then getting into bed with your honey and making some oxytocin. Afterward, enjoy a comedy and have a good laugh while diffusing lavender and vanilla in your room, and then end the day with a short meditation. Watch your happiness level soar, and listen to your soul sing!

> ### *1 Corinthians 6:19–20 (ESV)*
> *Or do you not know that your body is a temple of the Holy Spirit within you, whom you have from God? You are not your own, for you were bought with a price. So glorify God in your body.*

## Happy Telomeres

At the end of your chromosomes is a region of repetitive nucleotide sequences called telomeres. Current, cutting-edge research has shown that telomeres help prevent deterioration of your chromosomes. Which implies, that having longer telomeres will help defy aging. Sweet!

How do we have longer telomeres? Well, we increase our happiness, of course. The positive correlation between happiness and longevity is all we need as encouragement. Turn the clock back one smile at a time!

## Smile Biology

Speaking of smiling, did you know that smiling changes your brain?

Your brain takes notice every time you smile—it's like throwing a little exultant party in your brain. The more you smile, the more feel-good hormones your body releases, resulting in a profound effect on your emotional experiences.

We know that smiling improves your mood, thus reducing stress and blood pressure and boosting immunity. In the study *Grin and Bear It: The Influence of Manipulated Positive Facial Expression on the Stress Response*, researchers have shown that your smile doesn't even have to be real, and it will still have a positive result in your brain and body. (Fake it till you make it.)

What's more, because people react very quickly to facial expressions (it takes just a fraction of a second for your brain to recognize and respond to emotional expressions in others), smiling can also improve other areas of your life. People who smile appear friendlier and more polite, approachable, and knowledgeable, and that all results in a professional and social advantage. Of course, smiling is also contagious. So get your smile on!

## Homeostasis and Happiness

Your body and brain seek balance. I like to think of this homeostasis as a thermostat. As you know, if you set the thermostat on your home furnace to seventy and the temperature goes two degrees above that, the heater will shut down. If the temperature moves two degrees below, the heater turns on. From sixty-eight to seventy-two is called a comfort zone.

The body also has a comfort zone. This can be demonstrated by observing the body on a hot day—it starts to sweat to try to cool off.

What is interesting is that we also seek homeostasis on an emotional level. As crazy as it may seem, a great deal of happiness, when we don't feel deserving - can actually lead people to subconsciously create situations to lower that happiness. Happiness can temporarily make a person feel uncomfortable if it is not his or her normal disposition.

Likewise, people who find themselves feeling "too" successful often sabotage that success. How many musicians or actors have you seen become extremely successful, just to turn around that sabotage all they have worked for? In the financial industry, we have found that many folks who inherit or win a windfall often make poor financial decisions and end up losing most if not all of the money within a couple years. This is not only due to lack of proper financial education, but also, because they don't adjust to a new level of financial well-being. They subconsciously sabotage themselves. So the challenge to becoming happier, more successful, financially fit, etc. is to learn to adapt to the mild discomfort created in such a situation. In other words, you need to increase your thermostat comfort zone.

Gay Hendricks calls this an "upper-limit" problem. In his book *The Big Leap*, he helps describes ways to raise our comfort levels. The good news is that it is human nature to adapt.

When working with my financial clients, I'm continually sharing with them the incredible nature that humans have to adapt. To demonstrate, notice the last time you received a raise. What did you do with that money? Did it go to something worthwhile or did it just evaporate away? Often if you make more money, you frequently spend it. If you make less, you adapt to the lower income and adjust your budget accordingly.

We adapt because our brains like balance and order. If what is going on doesn't match the order and the reality we perceive, then we can potentially create a problem or ascertain a solution in an attempt to get our external circumstances to match our internal feelings. This is because we try to create meaningful perception and balance in a chaotic world.

Let's put this in practice. Let's say I'm accustomed to earning $50,000 per year, but I find myself making considerably less. Well then, I become extremely motivated and find ways to bring myself back to the financial health I'm accustomed to (the RAS system kicks in big time). Here are just a few examples of folks who have been wildly successful, filed for bankruptcy, and then later earned their wealth back again: Abraham Lincoln, Henry Ford, Walt Disney, Milton Hershey, H.J. Heinz, and P.T. Barnum.

You sometimes see this homeostasis pattern work in the opposite direction as well. For instance, if I'm currently earning $50,000 a year, and that is where I feel comfortable. I work very hard to improve my financial life, and eventually make $100,000. If I am uncomfortable with my new success, I may subconsciously do things to sabotage my success and bring myself back to my original $50,000 a year comfort zone.

You want to recognize when you are doing this and to be OK with the discomfort so you can boost not only your happiness but your relationships, financial, and physical health as well. Set a new level on your happiness thermostat.

## Self-Love
Occasionally, when I find folks are self-sabotaging in the areas of finance, relationships, or health, I recognize that this

can be a comfort zone issue *or* it can also be a vaster issue: an issue of value or rather more precisely a lack of personal value. Some people don't value or love themselves enough to think they deserve loving relationships, health, or wealth. So they subconsciously disrupt any success in those areas. In these cases, I work with them on enhancing self-love.

As you will recall in chapter 2, I reminded you that it all begins with Love, and God is Love. We also know that because we are created in God's image, we are also Love. Consequently, love needs to start with loving ourselves first. If we don't love ourselves, it's hard to share love with others.

One approach I use to help others start the process of self-love is to have them close their eyes and get a visual picture of the person they love most in this world. Then I tell them to substitute that person for themselves when making decisions. For example: Would I want _____ (fill in the blank with the person I love most) to be in financial crisis? Of course not! I often have a client in a given situation imagine that it is her loved one, in the same situation; then I have her make decisions based on what she would want for that person she loves most. When she can connect and understand that she needs to focus on what she feels for the person she loves the most in the world and apply that same love to herself, then her world expands.

I also stress the importance of self-care. Nourishing oneself with good nutrition, proper sleep, healthy relationships, and setting aside time for oneself are all fundamentals of self-love. Taking care of yourself and loving yourself is not selfish—it's absolutely essential.

When you value and love yourself, you become happier, healthier, and often wealthier, and you are able to have amazing relationships because all love starts with self-love. You honor your soul and take care of your spirit by treating yourself with kindness, showing yourself appreciation, speaking to yourself lovingly, and being caring and compassionate to yourself. When you truly love yourself, your self-love will not change only you—it will change everything.

Chapter Notes ~ Highlights:

_____

_____

_____

_____

_____

_____

_____

_____

_____

_____

_____

_____

_____

_____

_____

_____

_____

_____

_____

_____

_____

_____

_____

_____

_____

_____

_____

_____

# 15

## HAPPILY GRATEFUL

There have been numerous studies on the positive effects of expressing gratitude and appreciation in your life, and on the resulting 25% + increase in happiness. To feel gratitude is to recognize the goodness in your life. You feel positive emotions that in turn improve health and levels of joy.

Expressing gratitude and appreciation is also another excellent brain primer. When you consistently look for those things in your life for which you are grateful, you tend to invite more good into your world.

I have a "happiness junkies" group that meets once a month, and we decided do an experiment about gratitude and appreciation. We called our project CAOA: Conscious Acts of Appreciation. Below is a brief synopsis of our experiment:

*Our project is to create and maintain a vibration of appreciation—appreciation for kindness, for beauty, for love, for all. We committed to doing daily conscious acts of appreciation (and encouraging others to do the same) for one week, thus creating an appreciation revolution, and then reporting those acts and the outcomes to each other.*

*We practiced various forms of appreciation and gratitude:*

*\*Writing notes of appreciation to teachers \*Writing notes of appreciation and leaving chocolate for coworkers and building cleaners \*Writing a poem to my husband of appreciation and love \*Showing appreciation to animals \*Leaving a positive review for a company and sending a note thanking the company for its fabulous service \*Making a gratitude salad for a coworker \* Giving flowers to a neighbor and thanking her for always being there \*Finding something every day to thank my husband for \*Putting a smile on the face of the gas station attendant who helped me by giving her a dark chocolate Dove candy*

*What we discovered:*
*…I thought I was showing appreciation for others…a gift to them…and what I've noticed is…it's really a gift to me.*

*…I have had amazing outcomes…The total surprise was that I'm the one who personally reaped the most.*

*...I was able to look for beauty and things to appreciate in my personal relationships and with others.*

*...I actually notice the things to appreciate instead of the things that drive me nuts.*

*...I am discovering the mutual joy and kindnesses that occur...it has been very energizing for me.*

*...My relationship with my husband has expanded with every word of gratitude that I shared with him.*

*...Wow, this giving appreciation to others, even when not in their presence, really does give as much or more to the giver!*

Our little project actually rippled out into our community, and we noticed the increase in joy not only in our lives but in the lives of so many others as well.

There are many ways you can start on your appreciation or gratitude journey. For instance, you can write letters of appreciation; you can start a gratitude journal and write three things you are grateful for every evening; you can commit to finding one person a day to thank and find something good about. You could do a perpetual gratitude photo each day, taking a photo of something you value, find beautiful or appreciate for 365 days. You can have jar of Thanksgiving; throughout the year jot on a piece of paper or card a note of appreciation for something you are thankful for and then on Thanksgiving enjoy reading your year of appreciation. You can practice gratitude at the dinner table; this was something we established when our children were little. We would ask, "What went well today?" This gave our little ones a chance to focus on the good in their day. The value that practicing gratitude and appreciation plays in your well-being, mental health and happiness is absolutely astonishing.

Remember that what you focus on grows. So when you focus on those beautiful people, places, and things in your world, you invite more of the same into your life.

### 1 Thessalonians 5:16–18

*Be joyful always. Pray continually. Give thanks in all circumstances, for this is God's will for your life.*

### Proverbs 15:13 (ESV)

*A glad heart makes a cheerful face, but by sorrow of heart the spirit is crushed.*

### Psalm 118:24 (ESV)

*This is the day that the LORD has made; let us rejoice and be glad in it.*

Chapter Notes ~ Highlights:

_____

_____

_____

_____

_____

_____

_____

_____

_____

_____

_____

_____

_____

_____

_____

_____

_____

_____

_____

_____

_____

_____

_____

_____

_____

_____

_____

_____

# 16

## HOLDING HAPPINESS

Staying happy in the midst of uncertainty is something that can be challenging for me. I'm a planner. I'm a gal who craves certainty. I want to know how something is going to transpire. Remember, I'm the one who tried to find absolute certainty in the Bible and spiraled as a result.

What I've discovered is that I need to embrace the unknown, to simply have *faith*. I let go of trying to figure it all out and started to trust and watch God work miracles in my life. When I approach uncertainty from a "what if" scenario, I'm much happier. What if God has something better in mind for me?

I've also learned not to be attached to *how* things will manifest in my life. I merely trust and believe and let go of the how, and then I sit back and watch the phenomenon of God's wonder happen. Let go, let God! When I let go,

I not only let go of the control, I let go of the fear, doubt, anxiety, and desperation.

Keep in mind that this does not mean I do not take action to fulfill my goals, dreams, and desires. I am very action oriented. I'm a doer. You'll find that most successful people are so, as a result of their positive habits, actions and willingness to do the work. I also recognize that the words I say, the thoughts I think, the beliefs I hold, and the intentions I take create my world, so I spend time and energy keeping these things in alignment. I'm simply not attached to *how* it will actually happen. By moving **from forcing to flowing** I leave the fine details of the *how* to God. If I focus too much on the nuances of the how, then I become overwhelmed and doubtful. Instead, by having faith and belief, I let God put into place the magic of creation—and it just happens! I do my part and move in the direction of what I'm trying to achieve, and then I let God take the wheel.

### Proverbs 3:5–6 (ESV)

*Trust in the LORD with all your heart, and do not lean on your own understanding. In all your ways acknowledge him, and he will make straight your paths.*

### Jeremiah 29:11 (NIV)

*For I know the plans I have for you, "declares the LORD," plans to prosper you and not to harm you, plans to give you hope and a future.*

Chapter Notes ~ Highlights:

_____

_____

_____

_____

_____

_____

_____

_____

_____

_____

_____

_____

_____

_____

_____

_____

_____

_____

_____

_____

_____

_____

_____

_____

_____

_____

_____

# 17

## ULTIMATE HAPPINESS

*You don't have a soul, you are a soul in a human body.*

*—Attributed to C. S. Lewis*

Quantum physicists explain that all of life, creation, and the universe is one large continuous expanding vibrating mass of pure energy and **light**. Once again, science has finally caught up with the teachings of the Bible.

### Genesis 1:1–4

*In the beginning, God created the heavens and the earth. The earth was without form and void, and darkness was over the face of the deep. And the Spirit of God was hovering over the face of the waters. And*

*God said, "Let there be light," and there was light.*
*And God saw that the light was good.*

The universe is fluid, fluctuating and built up by our individual and collective energies, not constant, firm and unchangeable. I imagine this as if I am but a drop of water in the ocean. I exist as an individual with my own energetic being, **and** I am part of the whole universe. Everything radiates its own distinctive energy signature and yet is also intricately interconnected. Therefore, for me, keeping my vibration high, as close to God/Love/the Divine as I am able, is ultimate happiness.

Personally, I believe having high vibration means being in a space of love, awe, joy, peace, grace, and gratitude. I also know that if I match the frequency—using my words, thoughts, and intentions—of what I want to attract, it will manifest in my life, because God created the universe that way. Ask, believe, and receive.

### Galatians 5:22–23(ESV)
*But the fruit of the Spirit is love, joy, peace, patience, kindness, goodness, faithfulness, gentleness, self-control; against such things there is no law.*

*Love is the Ultimate and Highest goal to which man can aspire. The salvation of man is through Love and in Love. -Viktor Frankl*

One of the tools I use to check in to be sure I am vibrating and staying with God and in a state of Love is my activity tracker.

My activity-tracker watch will vibrate and tell me to get up and move if I've been too sedentary. I'm not always in a space where I can get up and move (if I'm sitting with clients, etc.).

Before, when the watch would vibrate, it would make me cringe and feel as if it were yelling at me to get up off my booty and move. As a result, I would feel guilty because I couldn't or wouldn't at that time. It would remind me of all I wasn't doing for my health.

Now, when the watch vibrates and I'm not in a situation where I can move at that moment, I use it as a reminder to check in on my vibration. Are my vibration and heart where I want them to be? Am I in the space of love? What am I grateful for in that moment? So I use the tracker as a reminder to ask myself, "Do the thoughts, emotions, and beliefs I'm having right now belong in my life? Is this who I want to be?"

Since I also understand that I become my absolute best when I get past myself and stay in a state of love, I become more in awe of the future than I am of the story of the past. As a result, I attempt to live future reality now. What? I live my future reality now. I live the life I want to have as if it is already happening. And guess what? It is!

### Philippians 2:2 (ESV)
*Complete my joy by being of the same mind, having the same love, being in full accord and of one mind.*

### Shine Happiness
*This little light of mine, I'm going to let it shine—let it shine, let it shine!*

Shine as brightly as you can. When you shine, you allow the light to cast itself on others. While shining, you create a sort of divine energy, an increased vibration in the world. We all have God inside of us, and by shining, we shimmer His light, His love.

> *Our deepest fear is not that we are inadequate. Our deepest fear is that we are powerful beyond measure. It is our light, not our darkness that most frightens us. We ask ourselves, Who am I to be brilliant, gorgeous, talented, fabulous? Actually, who are you not to be? You are a child of God. Your playing small does not serve the world. There is nothing enlightened about shrinking so that other people won't feel insecure around you. We are all meant to shine, as children do. We were born to make manifest the glory of God that is within us. It's not just in some of us; it's in everyone. And as we let our own light shine, we unconsciously give other people permission to do the same. As we are liberated from our own fear, our presence automatically liberates others.*

> —*Marianne Williamson*

Discounting our accomplishments does not benefit anyone. You are a child of God—of course you are absolutely amazing. Don't try to dull that light. Allowing your unique light to sparkle is actually a tribute to God. God tells us that when we shine, we cast light onto everyone…So shine on, my friends, shine on!

### Matthew 5:14–16 (NIV)

*You are the light of the world. A city on a hill cannot be hidden. Neither do people light a lamp and put it under a basket. Instead, they set it on a lampstand, and it gives light to everyone in the house. In the same way, let your light shine before men, that they may see your good deeds and glorify your Father in heaven…*

### 2 Corinthians 4:6 (ESV)

*For God, who said, "Let light shine out of darkness," made his light shine in our hearts to give us the light of the knowledge of God's glory displayed in the face of Christ.*

### Daniel 12:3 (ESV)

*And those who are wise shall shine like the brightness of the sky above; and those who turn many to righteousness, like the stars forever and ever.*

Chapter Notes ~ Highlights:

_____

_____

_____

_____

_____

_____

_____

_____

_____

_____

_____

_____

_____

_____

_____

_____

_____

_____

_____

_____

_____

_____

_____

_____

_____

_____

_____

# IN CONCLUSION

My Dear Friends,

As I said at the beginning of this book, I'm an expert neither on the Bible nor on the brain, nor did I originate most of these concepts. I'm also not a medical or mental health professional, and this book should not be misconstrued as medical or mental health advice. I'm a lifelong student of God, love, and happiness. The information I've provided was obtained through years of study by following experts in neuroscience and positive psychology, and through many contributions from others and life lessons learned. This book is a simple summary of some of the principles I've learned. While teaching my workshops I'm able to spend a great deal more time on the neuroscience aspects, as I'm able to share videos from scientists and real-life examples that I'm not able to elaborate on in this short read. Each chapter could actually be expanded into an entire book within itself. I encourage you to continue your exploration into the tenets that resonate most with you.

As a coach, guide, and teacher, I've made it an ongoing practice to seek out this information, to apply it to my life, and to communicate it to others. I can think of nothing that brings me greater joy than seeing others discovering the power they hold in the creation of happiness in their lives. If you would like me to hold a Happiness Connection workshop for your organization, church, company, or wellness program, please reach out to me at SoulTuned@outlook.com. I also have a secular workshop option for businesses that primarily address the science of happiness/wellbeing/success and more importantly how to apply that science to achieve your goals, dreams and desires.

Additionally, I urge you to seek out someone who will help remind you of these theories when you need that extra encouragement. One of the most beneficial functions of coaching is that it helps you remember, when you *temporarily* forget, of the incredible power you hold.

Always remember that you are a blessed child of God and that, as such, you are worthy and were created and designed to be happy!

Shine on! Hugs, love, and happiness, Christine

# AUTHOR BIOGRAPHY

Christine Schader is an inspirational speaker, author, happiness coach and owns a financial planning firm. She teaches several workshops in the community and to organizations on the Happiness Connection and Financial Wellness. She views herself as a lifelong student of God, love, and happiness. Christine lives in beautiful Coeur d'Alene, Idaho, has been married for over thirty-four years, and has two amazing adult children. In her spare time you can find her hiking, swimming, and boating in the gorgeous Pacific Northwest, enjoying life with her friends and family, or clicking away at the keyboard on her next book.

Made in the USA
Lexington, KY
24 April 2018